Pale
as Real Ladies
Poems for Pauline Johnson

Pale as Real Ladies

Poems for Pauline Johnson

Joan Crate

Brick Books

CANADIAN CATALOGUING IN PUBLICATION DATA

Crate Taylor, Joan, 1953-
  Pale as real ladies

ISBN 0-919626-43-2

1. Johnson, E. Pauline (Emily Pauline), 1862-1913,
in fiction, drama, poetry, etc.   I. Title

PS8555.R37P3 1989   C813'.54   C89-095013-X
PR9199.3.C73P3 1989

Fifth printing, July 2005

Brick Books is grateful to the Brant Historical Society for permission
to use the photographs of Pauline Johnson reproduced here.
Thanks also to Joan de Kat for her assistance.

The support of The Canada Council and the Ontario Arts Council
is gratefully acknowledged by Brick Books.

Printed on Zephyr Antique Laid, sewn into signatures and bound
by Coach House Printing, Toronto.

Brick Books
431 Boler Road, Box 20081
London, Ontario N6K 4G6

brick.books@sympatico.ca
www.brickbooks.ca

This book is dedicated to Kamal, Evan, Jeunesse, and Jordan with love.

CONTENTS

I

II   Legends

Prairie Greyhound

Two a.m., travelling south from Prince Albert on the Greyhound, I press against the window. The man slumped beside me smells of dirty socks, and he snores. It's dark. Only the driver glows in a halo of electric light. On the other side of the window the trees will be growing thinner, more stunted. Huddles of green are replaced by frozen fields paler than winter yolks, colder, the colour of Charles Wurtz's hair. Pauline, you are with me. Your face stares through the bus window, and I no longer know where I end and you begin.

He was your second lover, Charles Wurtz. Your second Charles. You were left by both. Did you confuse him with the first Charles who left you? Absences with the same name? Dual shadows bruising your thoughts, always there, always gone, always aching?

Emily Pauline Johnson, Mohawk Princess, the Chief's youngest daughter. Poet, patriot, author, actor, lover, spinster, lonely. With your audiences, friends and admirers, your partner J. Walter McRaye, your white Quaker mother, your half-blood siblings Eva, Allen, and Henry; lonely still. Half-blood was your word, preferable to half-breed. Half this and half that. Tonight on this bus, I am half me and half you.

Your mother insisted you be schooled white, taught her spotless manners. Yet it was the mottled history of your father's people you recited, his pride you adopted, your grandfather's Indian name, Tekahionwake, you took. "Hey squaw," they called from the foot of the stage. These relics were not enough to protect you from voices in the dark.

From Chief Joe Capilano you learned the Squamish legends and translated them into English. Some say you altered them because you did not understand his language, were forced to converse in stilted Chinook. Others say you wanted to make the legends acceptable to your white audience. He was your friend you say. I reach for your face, scratch glass.

How I would have loved to see you perform: your war whoops, your buckskin and pelts, the scalp inherited from your grandfather swinging from your waist, your father's hunting knife. And the tafetta as well, the exquisite gowns you wore in London parlours, the satin shoes, the plumes and curled hair. I've seen photographs and always wondered how you managed the change in the space of a fifteen-minute intermission.

"Hey Babe!" someone calls from the back of the bus. I can make out the gleams of a bottle, jittering liquid, a thick hand. It's still difficult for a woman to travel alone at night. In the window you watch me. "Squaw," they called on the bus, the train. "Yes I mean you!" My eyes stare from the inside of the bus window outside, from the outside in, peering from dark to darkness.

I write poems for you. I re-invent you. It is not your words I want, your books of verse, your stories and legends. It is the sound of your voice, your breath cool on my cheek, your insistent geniality, your travel, your toughness, your pretense. And your loneliness, your stretched-thin days, desolation, illness, suffering. Your death. Under headlights, a thin white tongue unravels the night. A face shifts.

It is either you or me, Pauline.

I

See this necklace?
It is made from the claws
of a cinnamon bear that went mad
when her young were slaughtered.
These are my poems.
The words have been scraped clean
of death and anger,
and will shine in your mouth
like a string of white pearls.

In the closet under the stairwell

Eva and I play with porcelain dolls.
Their hypnotized eyes demand
doilies for their table,
embroidered pillows. Over
their flaxen heads dangle woolen haloes,
musty with the memory of Mother's angel arms,
and a sky of neon beads strung across
Father's smoke-skin coat.

We will not allow our brothers inside,
sweaty from games and thumping dance.
They lurk, too bright, on the other side
of our curtain door.

For ourselves we steal Mother's
tatted collars to subdue the riotous
dresses our grandmother stitched.
We curl our hair and dust talcum powder
over cheeks and eyelids,
turn pale as real ladies.

Boarding School

The classrooms are large,
the walls so white
they are barely visible.
A tall spinster stands before us
and reads poetry that floats and sinks
to our polished shoes in pools of ash.
White faces fold towards her thin words.
Teeth a slight chatter,
the sound of china cups and saucers
held in trembling hands.
Someone scampers down the hallway
and a blue shadow crosses the linoleum
to stab our lungs with longing.

We are barely alive.

The eyes of my classmates are glass
weights pressing paper.
I trace their pink globe hearts,
the opaque arteries that fade
in pale bruises—
line drawings in pastel
smudged at the edges.

I want to unzip my satchel
and rummage for a barley sugar candy,
wrapped hard in chirping paper.
I want to suck it, taste it
sweet and amber on my tongue,
but cannot move.

It is becoming difficult to tell
the white faces from the white

walls of the classroom.
It is difficult to see.
Everything is turning white or lighter.
Even the words sinking into sound
numb like snow on unmittened fingers.

Mother and Grandmother,

lumps of clay,
glazed yellow by the fire.
Their fingers speak furiously
to the cloth, the coloured threads,
tongues locked in languages
they can't exchange.

Pattern of the hearth dances over them,
rhythm of needles and entwining lives
stitched with threads of blood.

Their mothers' thighs and bellies
hold memories of slow combustion,
cup the fire's mouth.

Voices

come with the snow moon
and the axis in my body tilts north.

Switch on the electric light, Mother,
help me choose a gown to wear for dinner,
jewels to cover my throat.
My breasts are tips of darkness
penetrating these papered walls.
You must pull me inside
with your soap smelling hands,
the click of your tongue.

As I pin my hair and stain my lips
you talk of the new pastor,
his indifferent wife, and the terrible
price of vegetables this time of year.
The alphabet folds neatly in my ears like linen,
absorbs the gurgle of heart
and bone and freezing earth.

I follow the whisper of shoes
on carpeted steps and feel the bite
of your floral scent on my winter skin.
You smile blindly at Father waiting
below in his new suit. Dark fur
grows at his throat, his wrists.
He hears the forest floor
crack open and moan.
Sing for us, Mother.

We follow your lilting trail
to the dining room

after the ball is over
after the break of dawn
after the dancers leave, dear
and I glimpse her—my grandmother
at the open kitchen door.
She stares outside at tracks
that skirt the house in dark blue hunger.

Jigsaw

Coloured pieces, these children
with shooting hair and blurred feet
playing near the Reserve school.
Motions lock into place,
piece pictures, fly
them apart. Mouths open
the air, laughter snaps
into wild blackberry eyes
that fit together a world
from shacks, a hungry dog,
and a cold current of lights
pulling pulling beyond the fence line.

The Poetry Reading

Tonight let me tell you of
a world swallowed in one quick gulp
with only crumbs remaining,
while in one stale memory-corner
a small girl shivers on the steps
of a tar-paper shack.
Her daydreams are bruises behind her eyes,
oozing songs of suicide
children mouth in her unfinished womb.

Can you hear me?

Powdered woman in the first row
your plucked eyebrows creased with concern,
look at me, diseased,
scarred with smallpox,
seeping gonorrhea, lungs smothered with T.B.,
drunk,
pushed into a sewer, a reserve,
the weed-choked backyard
you never walk through,
listen.

I speak of a history
pieced from a jigsaw of flesh
torn from dumb tongues.
Under my skin
blood beats along roadways
barred with DO NOT ENTER signs,
walls of small scars.
I will not return to silence.
Do you hear me?

Hands twitter.
You rise to your feet.

Lovely Miss Johnson.
And will you have tea now?
One lump or two?

You dust biscuit from the corner
of your mouth, and I remain
onstage in front of you.
I stare at the pelts
hanging from my shoulder,
and sip from fine bone china.

Gleichen

A wash-out ahead
so the train stopped for four days
on the prairie near Gleichen.
We played cards, told stories,
dined in Frogmore and St. Cloud.
Silverware, linen and china
chattered in our hands.
Like a picnic some said.

Then the Indians came,
Blackfoot, with their horses.
One dollar, their fingers sang, to ride
across the prairie and lick the sun.
Teeth glinted with sky.
But one pony fell in a badger hole
and broke its neck.
Look, said the man from Detroit,
the Indians will eat it.
They eat anything, diseased and
unclean things. Fingers pointed like
sticks of candy, laughter slapped.
The Blackfoot watched us, eyes bewildered
by sun. They rustled dry grass, vanished
into the yellow land smudge.

The gray horse bloated before us.

The look

on their faces,
these women with husbands
and children, who fill
compartments on the train,
their expressions heavy
with the honey they had for breakfast,
their babies' new teeth,
a careless hand stroking their breasts.
Their lips never tremble
with words no one hears.
Across their mouths a bruise
perpetually heals.
They glance out the train window,
sigh. They cannot imagine
the miles and miles of empty track,
the dinosaur bones the train crawls over.
A husband speaks, a child suckles.
There is dinner, and other wives and children
to lock into their solid faces.

I watch them, my body
a hundred broken lines wavering
in the thick air they carry around them.

Photograph of Mother

A young woman in the kitchen, her face
bitten with guilt. She is making bread
and her white Quaker hands shape prayers
in the dough, spill haloes of flour
through window light.

Someone has come to take her picture.

She squeezes daydreams from the nights
he touched her and all her blood thawed.
Tiny ice splinters melt her eyes,
peel her paper face.
Her breasts are hills of snow
smeared with his love chant—
faint red splatters on the border of the print.
She wipes her mouth with white dust fingers,
tastes raw meat.

The shutter falls.

She keeps the framed photograph under her mattress
and will not bring it out.
It's as if she knows the frozen kitchen,
the airborne flour, the gray sphere of dough
cannot hide the secret white fluttering of her hands—
angel wings over his dark back.

In England

I

I recited in the parlours of the rich,
draped in silk donated by matrons,
my manicured nails snagging
tapestry covered walls.

It was the savage poems
they admired most:
> *They dared not walk*
> *In day and meet his deadly tomahawk;*
> *They dared not face his fearless scalping knife;*
> *So—Niyoh—then they thought of me, his wife.*

They crush around me as I bow my head,
palms sweating, these jewelled fingers,
the centuries-cold marble floors.

II

The three Indian chiefs

startled London—
bark-skinned men, the earth
trapped in their bodies.
They came for an audience
with the King and Queen
about the land their government
stole for its citizens.
And waited, believing in justice.

In the palace, their images upside down
light and spirit tracked them
in ceilings of lake.
The chiefs shrank, distorted.
Wind whispered through fir boughs
as the Queen walked. It was a house
haunted with other language.
Royal lips dropped phrases
in lace panels in front of them.
The chiefs grasped at each individual thread,
snow-blind to the need for appearances,
the repeated patterns, the white lace flakes
falling over wolf tracks.

III

One day I found Chief Joe Capilano,
red fox crowning his head,
but he spoke no English.
    Klahowya Tillicum
And we slip into the bastard tongue Chinook.
Quaint. The word creaks around us—
or is it paper in reporters' fingers,
the crisp London breeze?

Fish oil flings rancid from the old man's lips.

Story teller

Your voice
scrapes the bones of time.

At night by the fire, it is only you,
Chief Joe, who feels
a lost spring flood thirsty cells.
In the dark heat you find legends
once buried, now
damp on your dry lips.
Whisper to me and I will write you down.

I will run ink through your long wounds,
make your past flash like fish scales
under a sharp knife.
I will give names to the tricks of seasons,
tie your stories of beginnings to weighted ends
with my careful fisher's fingers,
lock your chants, spirits,
dances, your paint, your potlatches
into a language you can't speak.
I will frame your history
on a white page.

The Society Page

The photograph of you and me in a carriage,
a gray smudge on the society page.
In your hand a card,
mine reaching.

I no longer want to write I whispered—
the pen's administration of such savoury poisoning,
drip of verse dripping on verse, the swallow,
and your silhouette against the camera flash,
listening?
    Shadows of horses over us.

Take this Pauline

Someone writes poems about me,
words lying on the page, small corpses.
She is afraid of my moist breath under her wrist,
and ink mixing our veins.
She reels me into the late twentieth century
where I am quaint as the disintegrating
paper lace on the valentine you gave me.

My fingertips beaten from the newsprint,
my mouth resigned to your leaving
so hungry for the arsenic
in the bright apple of your mouth.
I waited, your arm a broken link in mine,
Charles, my husband-not-to-be.

As I wait now in someone else's hands
for another betrayal.

Charles, what shall I do

when I am hungry and your mouth
is no longer here to feed me?
I am a child in a forest you led me to.
The trees are long bars you
will slip through one day like a curse.
My mouth practises remaining open,
waiting for your bread-white body,
honey whisper.

When I am cold
if your hands no longer ignite
my skin, who will watch
my dance bend to ash
and still feel heat?
Already the forest closes
green eyes, drifts to sleep.
Your fingers trail memory-smoke
over our limbs. Snow
is in your eyes.

When I am dark
if you are no longer here
to open my bones to carols of light,
who will plant suns on my brow each morning
and shine stars through my eyes at night?
Days shorten.
Your flesh falters
against the marching winter sky.

Another Train Ride

It was the only light on
in that town the train
churned through at 2:00 am.

I thought of stale sheets
and migraines, someone sick
looking for aspirin and
a not-too-dirty glass.

But perhaps it was a new baby crying
and a weary mother lifting him to her breast,
or lovers holding the swollen moment
when they are no longer alone.

After the Beating

Father, I would not look
as Mother unbuttoned red
crusted cotton and a vase filled
with murky water broke
all down your chest.
Stems pierced skin.
I plugged my ears against
your mouth unhinged, sang
Row, row, row your boat
Gently down the stream

For days I did not watch you
in the bed—shapeless mud overflowing
your edges—or notice the flowering
of bruises transforming your skin
into an old quilt. How you stooped
against morning light, eyes
collecting sediment.

I would not come to your bedside
that last time when you called me
my mother's name.

The Death of my Father

Mohawk death wail
eddies the morning air
up and down the river banks
the mists cling to his absence.
George Johnson, Indian Chief, Father,
you leave me haunted
with myself.

It was the attacks that killed him,
the lead ball that broke both jaws.
Then years later, the six whitemen
who crushed his ribs and shot him,
and finally the Indian
who beat away the last years.
It was because of the whiskey
he would not allow on the Reserve,
because of the stolen timber,
because of his people's sinking
from consciousness to sleep.
He sleeps now, my father,
under a blanket of snow
and the house he built is empty,
mouthing the echoes of river.

Pen writhes in my mother's hand.
Paper crumbles her bleached days.
She sits at her desk and writes letters
to him, as if he will find them
in the fork of trees, in the yellow grass,
as if he will answer them with a longing
spelled out on the blank sheet of river,

the etch of bird wings
on the gray slate sky.

It is the endless scratch of pen
on paper I cannot bear.
Back and forth her letters tear
across my vision of him,
up and down the flowing margins,
eroding, erasing.

The Censored Life of a Lady Poet

My poems are an opaque window.
Through a frost of words
matrons catch the movement
of your head falling to my breast,
glimmer of sweat at curtained edges.

This is all I'm allowed—
allusions glimpsed through a child's sketch
in condensation—a circle, two eyes,
a smile that opens my reaching mouth,
the taste of peppermints on my tongue.

I recite in chilly town halls,
am given my take.
I open my voice a crack
and allow a plume of tepid verse
to tease the chapped skin of the audience.

During intermission my head clouds.
I press ice cubes to my temples
and think of the mosaic of fractures
on the milky dinnerware
in my mother's locked cabinet.

When my voice breaks
I sip distilled water,
my reflection imprisoned in glass—
lips gulping
at a sound freezing in my fingers.

Dearest Pauline,

These words enclose me in our shared paper skin.
I kiss the curve of your hand,
slippery sighs, tremors that seep in familiar
flourishes of ink, (the open parentheses
of your arms.

you know how I care for you

Paper cuts my eye/
Words rise like an army, march
into traps draped in boughs of apology,
death beds of flowers limp
on the cutting edge of your rejection.

It is for the best, Pauline

Lines tear you from my life,
hard strokes glib with insincerity,
love's legalese, and me,
a skeleton entombed at the top of the page,

Charles)

The doors you opened in me,

the rooms we decorated,
our unblemished hands hanging
floral print paper, spreading
eyelet lace with its open mouths
punctured by cherry wood.
I unpacked my hope chest, laid
out towels embroidered His and Hers
for you to soil, a heart-shaped cushion,
threw out moth balls and dried
petal sachets, loneliness
no longer intact. You
made a home in my body.
I call you, Charles, your footsteps
in the hallway—Charles!—
walking away.

The Party

for Allen Johnson

Allen took off his flannel suit
and dressed like an Indian.
Beads shot his chest, feathers beat
the air, a scalp swung at his waist
as he danced.

The boss's daughter saw night
press against the eyes of a hawk
as he climbed hungry through a savage skull
listening to the curve of earth, waiting
for the flutter of a heart in grass.

Quick, she turned to run
through a room crushed with people.
How brutal the noise,
the throb of bodies around her,
wings in her ears.
His flying arms against the ceiling light
cast shadows over her cheek.
She closed her eyes, felt
a mouse squeak in her throat,
fur blotting her screams.

As she fell,
starched petticoats encircled her,
white talons around her
arms flapping against the falling,
the clawing night.

Someone helped her from the floor,
guided her to a carriage.
In the lamplight, the muscled rumps

of the Clydesdales trotting
were Allen's drumming thighs.

Dropping onto her father's paving stones
she shattered.
All night she would not lay
her head on the feather pillow,
but walked the floors
in fear of winged white sheets.

After the party Allen was fired
from his white collar job at the bank.

Encounter While Fishing

Joined at the mouth, my reflection
and I ponder the cloudy river,
the wrinkled sky.
I cast a baited hook into my breast,
watch it sink through circles of light,
golden strings entwining the line.
Lips kiss lips in a watery smile,
eyes set lazily on my eyes.

Earth-wash layers of river and sky
flood my nostrils, my mouth.
I am upside drowning,
no distinction between blue and blue.
Hook lances whites of eyes,
leaps through open mouth
with a silver squirm of fish scales.

I paddle for land, dart through the forest,
flee your depths, gills, your taste
for raw meat and salmon roe.
I leave you Emily Pauline.
You leave me Tekahionwake.
A long gray cord of shore uncoils between us.

The Naming

I

Call me Tekahionwake,
the name of my great-grandfather.
I am no longer Emily Pauline.

II

The French named us *les sauvages*
feet like storms under beating
sky   the pounding forest ribs
     sauvage who madden the wolves

Abandoned cold
in in dry-wall and paint,
we spoon food from cans
and switch channels.
Weddings and funerals
march in and out of time
we measure in digits
and no longer watch the dirty sky,
the trees, or feel the pull
of seasons in our blood.
The wind grinds outside me.

III

Bill me as the Mohawk Princess.
Exhibit me buckskinned on a platform,
chanting, my skin bitten
by teeth, quills, clawed.
To have you hear my voice,
I will turn any trick at all.

More Letters to Father

Still, so long after his death
she writes—hunched woman in black,
ticking dark words across the page.
"Not many years and I shall be by your side,
Dearest George, for I am getting old."

Young she was, in gray,
fragile as smoked glass,
and him fitted in maroon velvet,
with a black silk top hat
when they married.
Crowds watched them enter the church,
carriage loads followed them after—
this white woman, this red man,
this lady, this savage—
a festival, a circus, their joining.

She was ill after the ceremony,
a shiver of gray against his shining.
He took her home on the train, home
to the Reserve,
and as she lay on the starched
white sheets, he brought her
a tray of fruit and tea
with a freshly cut Blackeyed Susan.
When he whispered I Love You his lips
were a cool outline in the flushing air.

She remembers more.
Beneath her vacant eyes
red, orange, spray from his fingers
as he touches her in the dark.
Glittering secrets fold themselves in her face,
her hands. In pockets of her mind
their bodies clash and sparkle.

But she will not speak of love,
this proper old woman.
She strings letters and phrases
in hidden bouquets that bloom
hotly behind her lips.

At her hard wooden desk,
gardens burn
through black and white pages.

Henry, you died alone,

a bachelor man, afraid
to touch perfumed skin
with your half-breed fingers.

You blamed Mother for that, the way
she taught us to be separate,
allowed no bone ridges or blood seas
to be explored. Our salted forearms hung
at our sides. There was no good-night kiss.
Loneliness was a word you could almost
taste, unpeeled lemon far too large,
slipping, lodged in your throat.

How cold you looked in the coffin.
I could not touch.

To Allen on his Wedding Day

What is it that kept us alone?
Our mixed blood, a man at the cocktail party
suggested, like ruined wine, white
tainted with red, the inconsistency.
He dropped his monocle to stare at me
intently with his near-sighted eye,
and I laughed, moved on to graciously
accept the comfort of strangers.

In my bed at the McLaren,
I pull blankets over my bobbed hair,
shiver with cold. My Charles had left
before I arrived, and winter
nights in Winnipeg a cold black wire
tying off each solitary nerve before dawn.

Does Eva tremble this way?
So proper she would not allow card games
nor drink, announced she would rather not marry.

When she left her fiancee, Mother's
white lips pursed her dark face.
And now, righteous, does she sleep warm?

We sat side by side, two sister
crows at Henry's bed, waiting,
could not weep.
There were no other visitors,
yet he would not permit a kiss of greeting,
cringed at the flutter of our hands.
His rooms were furnished with alabaster
statues, hovered snow-blind, fearful
of Spring. At night he awoke,

with mouthfuls of flesh, sweating,
choking on no one's name.

There is only you Allen,
with that woman from the Reserve
who would not let you alone.
Is there no shame? Eva muttered,
lips bitten permanently pale,
and me ice-splintered in this hotel room
with steam pipes that chatter
the numb night long.

I send you my best wishes,
dear brother, with your new bride
wild with heat.

Eva, my sister,

a sermon numbs your face.
You hand me a china cup clattering
roses, the snap of your arthritic joints,
and reach for the Bible. You
spew a hailstorm of damnation—
retribution—the hard bite
of each syllable
delicious in your mouth.
Your voice rises as you gaze
at the glimmer of frost
on the ceiling rafters.
How cold Eva, the rooms of your house.

Sipping tea
you shiver from inside a shawl
and I bury my sins safe inside me.
Black seeds sprout.

In your winter kitchen
a steaming jungle choruses my bones.

Early snowflakes

barely there, and I walk
in woods hung over from too much summer.
On those fat days my canoe slit
the river belly and I gutted
with my oar; slashes healed
without a scar. Sometimes I swam,
limbs striking striking the watery mouth
bloated with salmon roe.
Fish darted elusive and everywhere.
I flung my ripe body on the shore,
swatted mosquitoes and sucked
stalks of wild grass, insatiable.
Life indestructible
and I was so strong.

Today I jar roots and flatten dry seed pods,
a skin of clunking vertebrae and human stench
souring the weak autumn breath,
everything old and crumbling.

But to be those flakes dissolving
before they touch soil.
That ineffectual.

The Cariboo Trail

for Billy

by stagecoach the photograph trembles   or
is it my eyes through large drops of dew
glass fish bowls and this small planet
spinning in my palm
your brown hands on chipped leather reins
dip into the Cariboo   cottonwoods fill
along sprung elastic river banks
gurgle light through the plod of horse hooves
and meadows turning topaz on my eyelashes
"Lac La Hache" you call
            Trail that winds and trail that wanders,
            like a cobweb hanging high

take me down the gullet   the long smooth slide
into grizzly and cougar country
satan's bloody water when the salmon run
the coach sways into a blue cavity
over mountain gums to a tongue of scorched plateau
            Just a hazy thread outlining midway
            of the stream and sky
there is no end and I will not climb
into petticoats in the mornings   you said
something about the only frontier left
when we spoke last   was it yesterday?
you no longer shave and my last pair of shoes
skid down a ravine   I shoot supper barefoot   a grouse

wings snap in my jaws up and down the land-flesh
when I unpin my hair it rolls earth waves   you
rip open your shirt where the sun makes golden
smootching noises like crickets at dusk   oh listen
            Sob of fall, and song of forest are singing
            there together through the God-begotten nights

behind the larynx   the ear drum
aching hollows
and your eyes attached to distance
blind to me so close

The Family

for J. Walter McRaye

Train slithers across the land spine
and we are swallowed inside
the same slippery years.
In the closeness we squeeze a strange family
from worn mouths—
four elves, a cat, a cockroach and mongoose.
They appear over coffee in the dining car,
scrambling over your forearms
to suckle my unused breasts.
Guests drop rolls, knives speared with butter,
and flee from our table,
while we gaze vacantly out the window.

Mirages glide by like parched seas.

Cancer

I have never known
a heartbeat pounding my belly,
the rolling of life inside my life,
the seed, the root, sapling
ripping through my soil
for light.

But this, branching inside me
folds the field of my body
into mountains of blue pain erupting.
Mutant seed, gnarled black root
anchors me in darkness.

Burrard Inlet at dusk

tonight I walk into the ocean
too tired to do anything but bathe
too weary to be picturesque
to serve as an example   sick
of desiring justice   with my long brown hair
in sea water   I am every shade
and any shade at all

I will describe the sea to you
in an appropriate verse form.

Shells in my eyesockets, crabs
scrambling my throat.
Such a glorious sunken vessel—
a book of my poems—
come to rest on your coffee table.

during the recital I choke,

      press a lace handerkerchief to my mouth

      syllables hatch in my throat
      force jaws apart
      wet back wings
      burst through lips
      carry my voice over
      familiar lines

           But still he dances to death's awful brink
           The eagle plume that crests his haughty head
           Will never droop though his heart be dead.

      verses flap through air and I reach
      after them to the lamps overhead
      the darkened entrance
      at the back of the hall
      I tamper with hearing aids
      try to pull down this rhyme-flight
           Wilder and wilder still
      that leaves me behind   locked
      in a cage of wrinkle and bone

Last Request

They will fasten the locket
with your picture
around my neck, and you will lie
with me when I am dead,
as I lay locked and dying in you
all these hollow years.

Your memory aches
in abandoned cells.
I will take you prisoner,
chain you to my flesh, burn
your gray eyes to gray ash
blinking in wind.

> *Because you came, and coming wrote the song*
> *That slumbered through the years I was alone,*

you will be with me
when I am dead, my dear lost lover.

Last Words

I watch my mother's fingers
through the silver web of moose skin,
slice with her knife, pull out bones
bound with ligaments and
a pink blood vessel like a slug.

Some days I dream I am spread
just beneath the peel of river.
Pebbles are gripped in my fingers.
My pain is held shut with needles of light.
You ripple over my face, wash me
with your liquid body. You hold
the terrible lumps of my red meat
in your running mouth, and speak of love.
Your words fill me with death
clean and slender as reeds and water.

My arms, my throat and face dirty
the hospital linen. Visitors search
for invisible black and red ants
that battle through muscle and blood.
Tiny pincers rip, jaws lock and
I am over-run, my self devouring itself
while eyes greedy as disease
capture me.

There is a smell in this room.
Knots of green bone have been dug up
by a neighbourhood dog.
I watch him chew,
my small fingers wrapped around
school books plump with visions.

Drifting in and out of drowning,
I cannot tell dark or light.
The sun is buried in sea and the moon

is a face I know but cannot name.
It wanes, waxes to another face
staring through me.
I reach for watery eyes
and the nurse pulls the switch.
Night pockets collect in my throat,
my lungs, my breasts. A needle drills
into me and black oil gushes to the surface.
I am empty stone, colourless.

Sounds are different now.
They whistle down a hollow river,
gurgle in my ears.
I am not sure if I have spoken,
if anyone has spoken.

Verses shake like rusty nails
in a damp paper bag. Once I thought
they could hold together the structure
of my thoughts. I wanted to be
the builder of beautiful interiors,
then open the doors.

I see a sinking shack on a bank far behind me.
Termites chew through splinters and dry rot.
A girl sits on crooked steps and shivers
in the drizzle. Withered leaves
whimper by her in the wind.
She is damp and cold and lonely
and knows she always will be.

> I do not like the moose meat sandwiches
> my mother makes me for school.
> I hide them in my toy box, shut the lid.
> Inside they mold and fester.
> There is a smell in my room.

I am walking inside a river.
I am a young woman, my body lithe as rope.
Water uncoils a light
that pierces and blinds where
the pain used to be.
Light spins through me
a choir of light sings through me
and my dying foot-falls beat
ing beat
ing away.

I am a Prophet

These words I speak have been given
me by angels. Moon-faced, they fall
into sight at night and spread wings
of pine needles through my skin.
Stories appear down my arms, across
my legs, they wind my waist in red haloes.

I have been chosen by Tyee
to tell of the beginning. My flesh
is a series of writhing tablets.
Let me show it to you.
I will dance without veils.
My body is a voice.
Listen.
My feet tell the story of the lost tribes
who wandered in their own darkness.
When they reached the Promised Land
they did not know it, but fell
down its wet, green gullet,
emerged as ravens, whales, eagles.
You may see their names written across my toes
for just one dollar.

But wait!
There is more. Here, along
my thighs are the virgin births.
Sand coloured maidens bathed
in mountain streams, were filled with salmon roe.
Smolts swam in their bellies.
Move closer, hear
the swell of secret waters.
The women married totem pole carvers
and bore fishers who pulled in full nets.
Each night the mothers reconstructed
the bones, threw them back to the sea,

and the salmon lived again.
Stay,
I will let you touch their fins.

Here, on my breast, see this rusty wound?
A cross marks the time the stories
dulled and Tyee took a few name
and began to live somewhere else—
across the sea in a garden where the plants
grow at the feet of men and women
and not through the trunks of their bodies.
Yes, you may kiss it.
Our garden was cleared,
and spirits shrank, hid in glass cages,
their moon faces darting through golden
liquid to burn hotly behind stupid tongues.

They will speak to you from my mouth
if you will just buy me a drink.
No, don't go yet!
You haven't seen it all.
For ten bucks I will show you
every scar on my body.
Another ten, you can make your own.
I will dance for you in a veil
of red waterfalls.
Stay, I am a prophet.
Angels visit me at night with pen knives.

II

Legends

It is a history, old man, that unwinds
from your long tongue glistening
in my stillborn brain. Tell it to me
so I might climb words back to a beginning.

Beaver Woman

I

All winter long there is nothing
but a membrane of ice over the pond
and the beaver lodge like a white breast
solid with unyielded milk.

I watch from the doorway
of our cabin, wait
for your feet breaking snow
from the north forest to me.

The nights are moonless and
the beaver lodge cataracts my sight.
Even when I close my eyes it remains
milk white, glowing.
I flatten my body on skins, press
into the memory of your brown hand.

In my womb, small animals unfurl.

II

Spring shuffles but your footprints
remain empty.
I grow pleas on branches, hang
them over my outstretched arms
dappled with buds and sunlight.
My mouth fills with longing.
The beaver lodge stirs and breathes.
I penetrate the pond, slide
over mud, through reeds and nesting birds,
algae plugging my nostrils,
the smell of your loins.

The fur of beaver kittens is warm
even in the darkest waters,
and I cling to them when the moon is thin
and the sky white with the cold fire of stars.

III

And now you come beckoning me
with your human hands, your feet
accustomed to walking green ferned trails
plant on the shore and I gaze up
to the earth in your eyes.

You must come into the water, husband
with your words that grind like teeth
in your jaws. My tongue longs
to stutter in the hollow of your neck.

If only the winter had not been so long
with nothing left alive but me
and a dark heart pulsing
beneath the beaver lodge.
I suckled hope from the movement of wind,
and a raven's call shadowing white.
Snow drifted through my veins until I sank
beneath the descending prayers of trees.

Come into the pond with your shivering lips.
I drink meaning.
Sink.
Nothing displaces me from these water-changes
but your man's flesh,
my woman's hunger.

Blue Sky how you won your wife

with secrets from the shaman.
She slept in her sealed tent,
oblivious of you, your longing,
and dreamed
your penis disembodied
bird-stretched to the moon
sweeping home to a midnight nest.

Beating wings awoke her—
heart beating feathers against her thighs.
A hard beak searched for food
through silken branches,
lifted her, struggling to fly.

Beneath the cool surfaces of skin,
where your words would not reach,
flames fluttered, charred her brown skin.
Thirsty-lipped through night
she wailed your cool name
  Blue Sky
  Blue Sky
Husband

Complacent man, now the gust
from your great wings
simply fans the flames
and your new wife never sleeps, burning
her lifetime with desire.

Woman who married a ghost

taken to the land of her new husband
her fingers lap island edges   plunge
to sea bottom debris and
slippery fish that dart between her thighs
she closes her eyes   feels
the muscle   bone   sinew
of his body swimming in hers   oh woman
there is nothing at night but
the empty net of your desire
don't you see
at morning his head a grinning skull
and no one to hear your screams
from a flesh and bloody throat

she writes words in sand
that swallows their meaning   wanders
the beach   sees bones and ashes
that were children playing by fire
          perhaps she's dreaming
perhaps she was dreaming before
when they were whole and human
when she was a new bride
one shoulder, her hips bear the marks
of her husband's hands   she cannot
remember his eyes   cannot see
          woman who married a ghost
nothing exists but his absence
and your beating heart sinking
in some imagined sea

Wife of Son of the Sea

Young woman cleaning salmon on a rock
counts her silvery selves multiplied on scales.
She probes a knife into flesh,
looks into water and glimpses liquid
eyes lapping her knees.

Waves pummel her mouth, her ears,
her deep earth eyes. She is a network
of channels, screaming—the gurgle
of a hooked fish—
and the Son of the Sea
drops fathoms deep inside her
drowning.

Possessed by tides, her heart
breaks along the salt line.
Between liquid and solid she's pulled
with nowhere to fall but in.

Landbound father, she grapples
with fingers and drifting memory
for your deliberate walk, your sweat, your skin
windbruised bark rough under her cheek,
and sinks like stone.
In beating fingers she holds the sea body,
hair rising in kelp ribbons
to the corrugated edge of dawn.
Wife,
sea daughter, we beat drums,
wave drenched limbs, try to touch
you, undefined as our belief.

Siwash Rock

stands ankle deep in water,
a man turned stone by the Changer.

In a cave his two wives wait for him
to return and push away the boulder
that blocks their entrance.
Their eyes are white quartz pebbles
that roll through shadow, strike
against his absence again and again.
Searching hands clatter together, withdraw,
the knuckles raw, palms dull
with the memory of his muscled body rippling
in waves of August sun under their touch.
They want to move mountains, to take him
back into the warmth of their stone womb.
Their voices scrape at his name,

lost lover
come home, come home to me.

My brother saw the first sailing ship

as he crouched on a rock ledge high
above the beach. The moon's ship,
ghost flesh breast billowed against light.

In the morning the ship dropped to the sea
surface with its cargo of moon children,
white as their mother's winter anguish.
Moon-skin hands scooped food
from shining discs,
pieces of the moon.
We traded sea otter furs
so that we might have them, hang them
dazzling from our lodges
to daunt the sun.

Moon children,
our chiefs dance for you on carved canoes,
spread eagle down to soothe angry waters.
High above in your ship, you watch us
with nightblind eyes.

I look into a piece of the moon
and see the dirty smudge of my reflection.
I fling it over water, watch it spin
the sky, glinting cloud
and hawk wings plucked suddenly
by the pale hand that catches it–
tin plate–
tearing the moon from sky.